Pebble® Plus

Physical Science

All About Temperature

by Alison Auch

CAPSTONE PRESS
a capstone imprint

Pebble Plus is published by Capstone Press,
151 Good Counsel Drive, P.O. Box 669, Mankato, Minnesota 56002.
www.capstonepub.com

 Books published by Capstone Press are manufactured with paper
containing at least 10 percent post-consumer waste.

Library of Congress Cataloging-in-Publication Data
Auch, Alison.
  All about temperature / by Alison Auch
    p. cm.—(Pebble Plus. Physical science)
  Includes index.
  ISBN 978-1-4296-6608-4 (library binding.)
  1. Temperature—Juvenile literature. I. Title.
  QC271.4.A829 2011
  536'.5—dc22

2010034308

Summary: Simple text and color photographs introduce temperature, including how thermometers work and the Celsius
and Fahrenheit scales.

Editorial Credits
Gillia Olson, editor; Veronica Correia, designer; Eric Gohl, media researcher; Laura Manthe, production specialist

Photo Credits
Alamy/Eric Chahi, 19
Capstone Studio/Karon Dubke, 7, 9 (all), 20–21 (all)
iStockphoto/Maria Pavlova, 1
Shutterstock/Armin Rose, 17; Junial Enterprises, cover; Karla Caspari, 11; Mandy Godbehear, 5; Rob Marmion, 15;
    Roman Sigaev, 13

Note to Parents and Teachers

The Physical Science series supports national standards related to physical science. This book
describes and illustrates temperature. The images support early readers in understanding
the text. The repetition of words and phrases helps early readers learn new words. This book
also introduces early readers to subject-specific vocabulary words, which are defined in the
Glossary section. Early readers may need assistance to read some words and to use the Table of
Contents, Glossary, Read More, Internet Sites, and Index sections of the book.

Printed in the United States of America in North Mankato, Minnesota.
092010
005933CGS11

Table of Contents

What Is Temperature?

Have you ever been outside on a hot summer day? If so, you know about temperature. Temperature tells us how cold or hot something is.

How a Thermometer Works

We use a thermometer

to measure temperature.

A thermometer's numbers and

lines stand for degrees. The

symbol ° also stands for degrees.

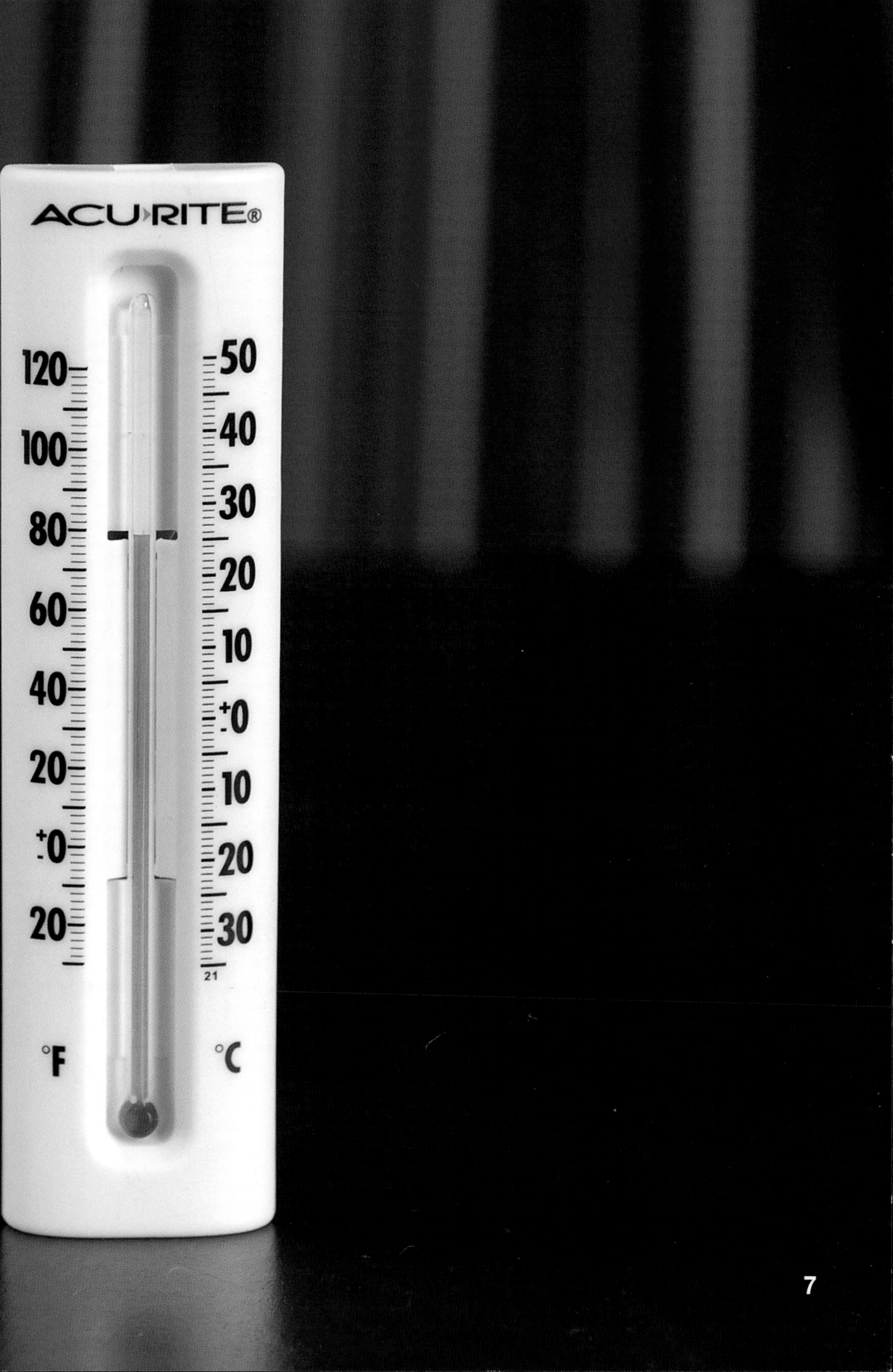
ACU-RITE®
120
100
80
60
40
20
±0
20
50
40
30
20
10
±0
10
20
30
21
°F
°C

In the thermometer is a liquid. As the liquid warms, it expands and moves higher up the tube. As the liquid cools, it shrinks and drops lower.

Celsius and Fahrenheit

Celsius and Fahrenheit are two

ways to measure temperature.

In the Celsius (C) scale,

water freezes at 0°.

Water boils at 100°.

In the Fahrenheit (F) scale,

water freezes at 32°.

Water boils at 212°.

To compare scales, water

freezes at 32°F and 0°C.

Temperature Facts

Temperature helps us measure important things. Most people have a body temperature of 98.6°F (37°C). A higher temperature can mean illness.

15

Some places are too cold for people to survive outside. In Antarctica the temperature was once measured at 128°F below zero (-90°C).

Some places get very hot.

In 1922 the Sahara Desert

reached 136°F (58°C).

It was the hottest air

temperature ever measured.

Make a Thermometer

What You Need

- 12- or 16-ounce (355- or 444-mL) plastic bottle
- food coloring
- water
- clear plastic straw
- modeling clay

1 Put five drops of food coloring in the bottle.

2 Fill the bottle 1/3 full with cool tap water.

Hold the straw in the bottle so it's in the water but not touching the bottom. The top of the straw should stick out of the bottle. Mold clay around the straw to seal the top of the bottle.

3

Hold the bottle in your hands for a few minutes. The heat in your hands will warm the liquid in the bottle.

4

Watch the liquid in the straw. The liquid goes up! The liquid in thermometers works in a similar way.

5

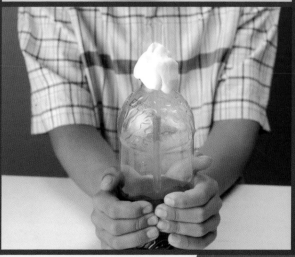

Glossary

boil—to heat water or another liquid until it bubbles

degree—a unit for measuring temperature

expand—to get larger

freeze—to become solid at a low temperature

liquid—a wet substance that takes the shape of its container

measure—to find out the size or amount of something

shrink—to get smaller

Read More

Doudna, Kelly. *Super Simple Things to Do with Temperature: Fun and Easy Science for Kids.* Super Simple Science. Edina, Minn.: ABDO Pub., 2011.

Manolis, Kay. *Temperature.* Blastoff! Readers: First Science. Minneapolis: Bellwether Media, 2008.

Royston, Angela. *Hot and Cold.* My World of Science. Chicago: Heinemann Library, 2008.

Internet Sites

FactHound offers a safe, fun way to find Internet sites related to this book. All of the sites on FactHound have been researched by our staff.

Here's all you do:

Visit *www.facthound.com*

Type in this code: 9781429666084

 **Super-cool stuff!** Check out projects, games and lots more at **www.capstonekids.com**

Index

Word Count: 181
Grade: 1
Early-Intervention Level: 22